Original title:
Chill of the North

Copyright © 2024 Swan Charm
All rights reserved.

Author: Kätriin Kaldaru
ISBN HARDBACK: 978-9916-79-564-4
ISBN PAPERBACK: 978-9916-79-565-1
ISBN EBOOK: 978-9916-79-566-8

Twilight's Embrace in the Silence of Snow

The sky drapes soft in violet hue,
As snowflakes dance, a gentle view.
Whispers of night in the frosty air,
In twilight's embrace, serenity rare.

Trees stand tall in their cloaks of white,
Holding secrets of the coming night.
Silence settles like a tender kiss,
In the hush of snow, a moment of bliss.

Footsteps muffled, the world is still,
With every flake, hearts start to thrill.
The moon peeks out, a watchful eye,
As shadows linger, and time drifts by.

A lantern glows with a warm, soft light,
Guiding lost souls through the tranquil night.
Memories linger like the stars above,
In the silence of snow, we find our love.

As dawn approaches, the colors blend,
Embracing the night, as dreams transcend.
In twilight's hold, we find our way,
Through the softest whispers of winter's day.

Northern Lights' Soft Caress

Dancing lights in the starry night,
Colors weave in a cosmic flight.
Whispers of a world untold,
Nature's beauty in hues of gold.

Beneath the green and violet sky,
Dreams awaken, as spirits fly.
In silent wonder, hearts collide,
With every shimmer, stars confide.

Shadows in a Snowy Glow

Blankets of white calm the ground,
In the stillness, peace is found.
Footprints lead in a secret dance,
Glistening softly, winter's trance.

Whispers echo through the trees,
Carried gently by the breeze.
Shadows flicker, play, and sway,
As day gives way to end of day.

The Winter's Breath

Frosted air in the morning light,
A chill that brings the world to white.
Every exhale, a cloud of grace,
Nature's rhythm, a slow embrace.

Mountains high dressed in gleaming snow,
Silent valleys where soft winds blow.
In frozen stillness, hearts ignite,
In winter's breath, life feels so right.

Glacial Serenade

In glacial caves, the echoes sing,
Melodies of the ice, they bring.
Crystal formations, intricate lace,
Softly shimmering in their place.

A symphony of nature's art,
Frigid whispers that warm the heart.
Harmony in the coldest night,
Glacial serenade, pure delight.

Birches in the Frost

White branches glisten bright,
Underneath the silver light,
Whispers of the winter air,
Nature's art, a scene so rare.

Frozen boughs with gentle sway,
Echo thoughts of yesterday,
A touch of calm, a hush profound,
In this tranquil, frosty ground.

Footsteps crunch on icy trails,
Nature's beauty softly pales,
Birches standing proud and tall,
Guarding secrets of the fall.

Glistening beneath the stars,
Memories held in the bars,
Of frost that kisses every tree,
In silent wonder, we agree.

Night enfolds the world in peace,
As frosty breaths begin to cease,
Birches whisper to the dawn,
In their grace, we are reborn.

The Lang Syne of the Frozen

Echoes of the past resound,
In the chill that wraps around,
Time has stopped, yet we hold tight,
To the warmth in the cold night.

Frosty fingers trace the air,
Words of friendship linger there,
Toast to times both good and wane,
Lang syne sung through frosty pain.

As the stars begin to fade,
Memories in silence laid,
Faces gleam in winter's glow,
Together, we let kindness flow.

Snowflakes swirl in fleeting dance,
A soft spell of sweet romance,
In the silence, hearts align,
Forever in the frozen time.

Celebrate the tales we've spun,
Underneath this frozen sun,
In the heart of winter's song,
We find where we all belong.

Songs of the Sullen Skies

Gray covers drape the distant shore,
A murmur deep, a quiet bore,
Sullen skies whisper their tune,
Beneath the watchful, waning moon.

Clouds gather, heavy with thought,
In this mood, our hearts are caught,
Eyes cast up in deep dismay,
As shadows stretch and fade away.

Each drop of rain sings a sigh,
In harmony, as loves comply,
Melody drifts on the breeze,
Like frozen breath in winter's freeze.

Beneath this vast and brooding dome,
We search for solace, find a home,
Together in this grayish shroud,
Sullen songs echo, soft yet loud.

Yet in the gloom, a light will break,
A promise found, a chance to wake,
Songs of hope in somber skies,
Will lift our souls as the darkness flies.

Whispering Pines and Spruce

Tall and proud, they stand in line,
Whispers echo through the pine,
Breezes carry tales unique,
Nature's song, soft and mystique.

Spruce embraces winter's chill,
In peaceful woods, time stands still,
Branches sway with gentle grace,
A warm heart in nature's space.

Silent woods, a breath of peace,
Echoes linger, tensions cease,
Among the trees, our spirits rise,
In the calm beneath the skies.

Snowflakes dance on emerald leaves,
A world of quiet dreams it weaves,
In whispering winds, we confide,
Each secret held, none denied.

Among the pines, our worries fade,
In a refuge nature made,
Whispering tales of hope and light,
Through the silence of the night.

The Arctic's Gentle Breath

Whispers of the icy breeze,
Dance among the silent trees.
Snowflakes twirl with graceful ease,
Nature's calm, our hearts appease.

Stars adorn the velvet night,
Glowing softly, pure and bright.
Underneath this tranquil light,
Frosty dreams take gentle flight.

Waves of white in moonlit glow,
Tales of warmth in frost do flow,
Echoes of the earth below,
In this realm, all worries slow.

An aurora paints the skies,
Colors shimmer, nature sighs.
In this place where magic lies,
Time stands still as daylight dies.

Home to creatures, strong and bold,
Silent stories to be told.
In the arctic, bright and cold,
Beauty pure, like dreams of old.

Frozen Echoes

In the stillness of the night,
Chill of frost, the world feels right.
Echoes linger, soft and light,
Whispers carried in moon's flight.

Frozen lakes like crystal glass,
Reflecting dreams that swiftly pass.
In this moment, time's a lass,
Held so tight, as shadows cast.

Mountain peaks in snow draped white,
Guard the secrets held so tight.
Nature's breath, both small and slight,
Lingers softly, pure delight.

Winds will sing a haunting tune,
Underneath the watchful moon.
In this place, where spirits swoon,
Stars will guide as night meet noon.

Frosted branches painted glum,
Yet in silence, life becomes.
Nature's pulse, a distant drum,
In frozen dreams, our hearts succumb.

Lullaby of the Frost

Softly now, the night descends,
In the chill, the silence bends.
Nature hums as daylight ends,
Lullabies the frost extends.

Snowflakes dance on whispered breeze,
Falling gently from the trees.
Each a note of winter's keys,
Playing tunes that bring us peace.

In the quiet, shadows stir,
Every breath begins to blur.
Stars above, a silver spur,
Nature's song, a soothing purr.

Cradled by this love of cold,
Stories from the past unfold.
Whispers from the brave and bold,
In this night, the heart takes hold.

So listen close, let worries cease,
In the frost, we find our peace.
Nature offers sweet release,
Lullabies that never cease.

Shiver in the Twilight

Crepuscular light bids farewell,
Softest shadows softly swell.
In the hush where whispers dwell,
Secrets only night can tell.

Frosty air caresses skin,
Nature's laughter, thick and thin.
Moonlight bathes the earth within,
As we gather, warmth begins.

Glimmers dance in twilight's glow,
Through the grove, the cool winds blow.
In this place where silence sows,
Time meanders, soft and slow.

Each heartbeat matches night's refrain,
Echoes deep, yet never plain.
In our shiver, joy and pain,
Blend together, like the rain.

Here in twilight's gentle clasp,
Life's sweet moments, we must grasp.
As the world begins to gasp,
In the stillness, love will clasp.

Ghosts of the Snowy Past

Whispers in the frost-filled air,
Echoes dance without a care.
Footprints lost in glistening white,
Memories fade like day to night.

Shadows linger, tall as trees,
Stories told in chilled, soft breeze.
Silence blankets every sound,
In the snow, lost dreams are found.

Frozen tales from ages old,
Secrets in the ice unfold.
Glimmers of the lives once led,
In the cold, we see the dead.

Frosty veins in streams of time,
Cascades of old in snowy rhyme.
Embers of a past unbound,
In each flake, a love profound.

Ancient hearts beneath the chill,
In the white, a haunting thrill.
Ghosts that roam in winter's breath,
Dancing close to whispers of death.

Breath of the Polar Seas

Waves collide with icy shore,
Echoes of the ocean's roar.
Beneath the frost, a world alive,
Where ancient sailors' spirits thrive.

Ripples shimmer under light,
Guiding boats in the twilight.
Fur-laden dreams of journeys far,
Navigating by the northern star.

Frosty crowns on ocean's crest,
In the chill, the heart finds rest.
Breath of the seas, crisp and clear,
Songs of the deep, all we hold dear.

Tales of storms and whispered gales,
Tides that tell of lost, bold trails.
Every wave, a tale to share,
In the depths, the secrets flare.

Frozen currents that glow bright,
Underneath the moon's soft light.
Ocean whispers on the breeze,
Breath of the polar seas, it frees.

Threads of Ice in the Night

Starlit paths of silver shine,
Woven threads through time align.
Crystals dance in moonlit glow,
Whispers of the night's soft flow.

Frozen echoes, soft and sweet,
In the dark, the heart does beat.
Each step taken on the frost,
In the night, we find what's lost.

Nighttime stories thread the air,
Whispers hang without a care.
Underneath the arctic sky,
Dreams take flight, and spirits fly.

Wanderers of the silent dark,
Guided by the cold night's spark.
Ghostly trails that lead us near,
In the dark, we conquer fear.

Threads of ice, a silken path,
Through the night, we share the laugh.
In the chill, our hopes ignite,
Boundless joy in threads of night.

Songs of the Frigid Pathways

In the silence, songs arise,
Carried forth on chilly skies.
Footprints tale a rhythmic dance,
On the ice, we find our chance.

Frigid winds in harmony,
Nature sings a symphony.
Every step a note we play,
In the cold, we find our way.

Echoes of the past resound,
In the blanket of the ground.
Whispered tales of hope and loss,
In the snow, we count the cost.

Melodies of glistening stars,
Songs of dreams that roam so far.
Riding waves of frosty air,
In the night, we pause and stare.

Pathways carved in winter's grace,
Every turn a warm embrace.
In the chill, our hearts confide,
Songs of the frigid pathways guide.

Nightfall in the Frozen Woods

The shadows stretch and grow,
Whispers weave through trees,
A chill breathes on the air,
As silence stirs with ease.

The moon peeks through the boughs,
Casting silver on the ground,
The night wraps round the woods,
With magic all around.

Each branch adorned with ice,
Glistening in the dark,
Nature dons her jewels,
Transforming every park.

Footprints mark the snow,
A trail of quiet dreams,
As darkness dips its brush,
Into night's soft scheme.

Amongst the frozen hush,
Life holds its breath in peace,
And in the heart of cold,
The world's wonders never cease.

A Tapestry of Frost

A canvas dressed in white,
Threads of ice interlace,
Nature's art unfolds,
With delicate embrace.

Each flake a whispered tale,
Beneath the moon's soft glow,
The world, a masterpiece,
In winter's gentle show.

Branches wear a cloak,
Of frost that sparkles bright,
A tapestry of dreams,
Woven through the night.

Quiet lingers in the air,
As starlight starts to play,
Every shimmering touch,
Transforms the world to gray.

With every breath of wind,
The winter whispers low,
In this frosted realm,
Time begins to slow.

Frosted Footprints

In the still of winter's grasp,
Footprints lead the way,
Marks of stories left behind,
In the soft, cold clay.

Each step tells a secret,
Of journeys far and wide,
Through the frosted wonder,
With the night as our guide.

The moonlight softly shines,
On paths that weave and wind,
A map of fleeting moments,
In the snow we find.

Through shadows and silence,
We wander, hearts aglow,
Frosted footprints linger,
In the chill below.

And when the dawn emerges,
The trace will fade away,
Yet memories remain bright,
In our hearts they'll stay.

Stars Over the Snowfield

A blanket of pure white,
Drapes over the land,
Stars above like diamonds,
In the night's soft hand.

The silence swells with light,
As beauty takes its form,
Each glimmering point of hope,
In darkness stands warm.

The snowfield stretches wide,
Reflecting every beam,
A dance of twinkling orbs,
In winter's frosty dream.

The air is crisp and clear,
Breath mingles with the chill,
Underneath the vast expanse,
The heart finds peace, be still.

For in this fleeting moment,
All worries drift away,
As stars shine down upon us,
In the night's embrace we stay.

Frosted Whispers

Whispers dance on frosted air,
A gentle chill beneath the stare.
Moonlit glimmers, soft and bright,
Casting dreams in silver light.

Snowflakes fall in silent grace,
Covering all in a soft embrace.
Nature breathes in hushed delight,
Wrapped in calm, a soothing night.

Branches wear their crystal crowns,
While the world beneath them frowns.
Yet beauty shines in frigid sighs,
Frosted whispers 'neath winter skies.

Time stands still, the night grows deep,
While the frozen earth does sleep.
Within the silence, hearts can find,
A sacred peace, a gentle mind.

Stars above begin to fade,
In the pastel light, dreams are laid.
Frosted whispers softly fade,
In the warmth of dawn's cascade.

Winter's Embrace

The world is wrapped in white and chill,
A canvas set, serene and still.
Trees stand tall with branches bare,
Embraced by winter's tender care.

Footprints tracing paths unseen,
Through realms of quiet, calm and green.
Each breath a mist in frosty air,
A moment's pause, a simple prayer.

Chill winds weave their winter song,
Whispering tales of those long gone.
Nature's quilt, a pure delight,
Blankets all through longest night.

Stars are shining, bright and clear,
Guiding dreams that drift so near.
Winter's embrace holds all so tight,
In stillness deep, there shines a light.

With every flake that falls anew,
Painting earth in shades of blue.
Winter's embrace, both cold and kind,
Wraps our souls and frees our minds.

Beneath the Icy Veil

Beneath the icy veil, we tread,
On whispering paths where dreams are led.
Each crunch of snow, a secret told,
In nature's breath, the world unfolds.

Frosted breath of morning light,
Kissing the trees, a pure delight.
Every branch in white attire,
Sparkles bright like frozen fire.

Ripples dance on crystal lakes,
Where silence falls and stillness wakes.
A gentle hush, the air draws near,
Beneath the icy veil, we hear.

The world is cloaked, the day is small,
Yet still, a beauty captivates all.
Beneath the veil, the heart beats strong,
In winter's melody, we belong.

As twilight weaves the stars in threads,
Over snow-draped hills and sleepy beds.
Beneath the icy veil we sigh,
In winter's warmth, we learn to fly.

Silence of the Snowbound Pines

In pines so tall, the silence reigns,
Wrapped in white, like soft gold chains.
The world around is hushed and still,
As winter's breath gives hearts a thrill.

Moonlight casts a gentle glow,
On snowy paths where whispers flow.
Each flake that falls, a secret kept,
In snowbound pines, the forest slept.

Shadows dance in twilight's embrace,
While stars peek out in soft grace.
Branches sway to a timeless song,
In silence, they've been resting long.

Footprints linger, then disappear,
In the quiet, nature draws near.
The peace of snow, a soothing balm,
In winter's hold, a gentle calm.

After dusk, the world transforms,
In silent nights, the heart warms.
Among the pines, where snowflakes shine,
Whispers echo, pure and divine.

Whispers in the Dark of Winter

The night descends, a quiet shroud,
Where secrets breathe beneath the cloud.
Frosted limbs in silence sway,
As moonlight paints the world to gray.

A whisper weaves through frozen trees,
Carried softly by the breeze.
It tells of dreams wrapped in white,
And starlit hopes that pierce the night.

Footprints muffled in the snow,
Echo stories of long ago.
Each flake a message, brief and clear,
Of memories brought close and near.

In shadows deep, a stillness grows,
Where solitude and comfort flows.
The heart finds peace in this embrace,
As time stands still in winter's grace.

So listen close to winter's song,
In every note, you will belong.
For in the dark, there lies a spark,
A warmth to light the winter's dark.

Glistening Shadows of the Glacial Woods

Amidst the pines, the shadows weave,
A tapestry that dreams achieve.
Glistening crystal, bright and bold,
In nature's arms, a tale unfolds.

Each step a crunch, a soft refrain,
As sunlight kisses frozen grain.
The woods alive with whispers low,
The dance of silence, soft and slow.

Shadows stretch, embrace the light,
In fleeting moments, day turns night.
Every glimmer tells a tale,
Of ancient paths that will prevail.

A hidden world in icy hold,
Where stories of the wild are told.
Beneath the frost, life quietly stirs,
In glacial woods, where beauty blurs.

So wander through the silver scene,
Where every shadow holds a dream.
In nature's heart, find peace and grace,
In glistening woods, your sacred space.

The Stillness Before the Storm

The air hangs thick, a silent pause,
Nature holds its breath, because.
The clouds amass, a heavy gray,
As shadows gather, come what may.

Birds take flight with anxious cries,
In the stillness, tension lies.
A brooding sky, a trembling air,
Forebodes the tempest lurking there.

The world is hushed, on edge it leans,
As whispers dance in fading greens.
Each leaf and branch in quiet plea,
Awaiting what is yet to be.

A flicker brews, a distant sound,
As nature's fury spins around.
Yet in this calm, there's strength to find,
The promise of the wild, unkind.

For after storms, the skies will clear,
And in their wake, the heart draws near.
To know that life, through chaos, sways,
In stillness found, the heart obeys.

Snowy Owl's Watchful Eye

In moonlit night, so crisp and bright,
A snowy owl takes graceful flight.
With wings outspread, so soft, so wide,
It glides through shadows, naught can hide.

Its gaze, a keen and piercing light,
As quiet lands beneath the night.
Each movement slow, so full of grace,
In dance with silence, finds its place.

The world below, a canvas white,
Imprints of life, the hidden sight.
A watchful eye upon the ground,
In snowy depths, the prey is found.

With every flap, a snowy ghost,
It roams the realms it loves the most.
A guardian of the midnight hour,
In tranquil stillness, holds the power.

So let us learn from this wise flight,
To find the peace in darkest night.
For in the quiet, wisdom lies,
As snowy owl surveys the skies.

Journey Through a Winter's Dream

Softly fall the flakes of white,
Blanketing the world so bright.
Footprints mark the frozen ground,
Silent stories all around.

Trees adorned in crystal lace,
Nature's tender, frosty grace.
Whispers of the chill so deep,
In this dream, we drift and leap.

Stars above in velvet night,
Guide us through the soft moonlight.
Each breath clouds the winter air,
As visions dance without a care.

Warming fires and laughter shared,
Hearts entwined, none feeling scared.
In this moment, time stands still,
A sacred peace, a gentle thrill.

With every step, a story told,
In frozen hands, dreams unfold.
Journey onward, embrace the gleam,
Lost forever in winter's dream.

The Silence of Shimmering Snow

In the hush of falling snow,
Silent worlds begin to grow.
Every flake a whispered thought,
Nature's beauty, finely wrought.

Moonlight glistens on the ground,
A magic spell, profound,
Frozen stillness fills the air,
Capturing dreams laid bare.

Footsteps muffled, echoes fade,
In this realm, darkness made.
All around, a blanket white,
Enfolding us in pure delight.

Frosted trees, a spectral view,
Nature's canvas, ever new.
Breathe in deep the chilly peace,
In this quiet, find release.

The night whispers soft and low,
In the silence of the snow.
Rest your heart beneath the glow,
In the quiet, let love flow.

Frosted Whispers of the North

In the North where cold winds blow,
Whispers weave through silver snow.
Crisp air carries tales untold,
Of winter's magic, brave and bold.

Pines stand tall, adorned in white,
Guardians through the winter night.
Frosted breath, a fragile plume,
In this silence, nature's bloom.

Shadows dance in moonlit rays,
Guiding wanderers through the haze.
Each step sings of ancient lore,
In the stillness, we explore.

Tales of creatures snuggled tight,
As the world sleeps through the night.
Every flake a story spun,
Underneath the northern sun.

In this frost, our hearts align,
Drifting gently, intertwine.
Frosted whispers softly call,
Embracing winter, we stand tall.

Icy Echoes of Twilight

Twilight casts its icy spell,
As shadows start to softly dwell.
Light retreats from frosted ground,
In the stillness, peace is found.

Echoes of the day now fade,
Night embraces, unafraid.
Stars awaken, twinkling bright,
In the chill of approaching night.

Beneath the vast and open sky,
Silent wishes soar and fly.
With every breath, the cold ignites,
Filling hearts with winter's sights.

Time slows down in twilight's grasp,
A fleeting moment, we clasp.
Icy whispers kiss the trees,
Carried gently by the breeze.

As the world wraps up its day,
In quiet reverie, we sway.
Icy echoes softly chime,
In this twilight, we find rhyme.

Silent Serenade in White

Snowflakes whisper in the night,
A blanket soft, pure and light.
Trees stand tall, silent and still,
Nature weaves a magic thrill.

Footsteps crunch on frosty ground,
In this peace, no other sound.
Stars above begin to gleam,
Lost in wonder, lost in dream.

Moonbeams dance on frozen streams,
Echoes of forgotten dreams.
Every breath a cloud of white,
Wrapped in warmth, wrapped in light.

In the stillness, hearts can mend,
Time stands still, a joyous blend.
Find the beauty in the freeze,
Silent serenade with ease.

As night drapes her velvet cloak,
Whispers rise as firewood's stoke.
All around the world is bright,
In this silent, snowy night.

Shivers on the Wind

Cold gusts dance through barren trees,
Whistling softly on the breeze.
Chill embraces every soul,
Nature plays a frosty role.

Branches sway with whispered fears,
Carrying echoes of lost years.
The world dressed in icy hues,
With every gust, a change ensues.

Frosted whispers, secrets shared,
In its grip, no one is spared.
Through the night, the shadows creep,
Haunting dreams as silence weeps.

Snowflakes swirl like thoughts gone cold,
Memories wrapped in tales untold.
Windswept paths lead hearts astray,
Shivers on the wind, they play.

In this dance, we find the grace,
Of winter's soft, enchanting face.
Every breath a frosty sigh,
In the chill, our spirits fly.

Arctic Dreams in the Moonlight

Moonbeams cast a silver glow,
On the land where cold winds blow.
A world transformed, enchanted sight,
In the stillness of the night.

Glaciers gleam like ancient stones,
Echoing long-forgotten tones.
Whispers of a time gone by,
Underneath the velvet sky.

In this realm, the lost can roam,
Finding warmth away from home.
Every flake a story spun,
Underneath the midnight sun.

Frosty air, a sweet embrace,
Wrapped in night's serene grace.
In the hush, our dreams take flight,
Arctic wonders in the night.

With each breath, the world stands still,
In the moon's embrace, a thrill.
Awake we wander, hearts in tune,
Lost in arctic dreams, a boon.

Frostbitten Tales of Solitude

In the silence, stories grow,
Of ancient paths, of ice and snow.
Frostbitten tales, whispered low,
In the shadows, feelings flow.

Alone beneath the starlit sky,
Even echoes hum a sigh.
Lonely hearts in whispers meet,
In frostbitten tales, bittersweet.

Night unfolds its secret veil,
Each moment, a pensive tale.
In solitude, we find our way,
Through the night, into the day.

Bitter chill, yet warmth inside,
In these stories, we confide.
The frosty breath of time's embrace,
Leaves its mark, a tender trace.

As dawn brings light, shadows fade,
Yet the heart, a tranquil glade.
Frostbitten tales, forever hold,
The warmth of stories shared and told.

Frost-Kissed Memories

In the chill of dawn's embrace,
Whispers of the past take flight.
Each flake that falls, a fleeting trace,
Of laughter lost to winter's night.

Footprints echo on frozen ground,
Stories lost in a glistening white.
In silence, where no secrets are found,
Shadows dance in the soft moonlight.

Fragrant pine and icy air,
Wrap around like a forgotten song.
Time stands still in this frozen lair,
Where echoes of childhood still belong.

Underneath the twilight's sheen,
Hope glimmers like a distant star.
In memories, where love has been,
Frost-kissed, never too far.

We walk among the trees of old,
Each branch adorned with crystal delight.
In the warmth of tales retold,
We find our peace in the winter's night.

The Haunted Silence of Winter Woods

In the woods where shadows crawl,
The winter breathes a haunting tune.
Branches whisper, softly call,
As cold winds wail beneath the moon.

Footsteps crunch on frozen leaves,
Silent echoes of days long past.
In solitude, the spirit weaves,
A tale of time that slipped too fast.

The air is thick with secrets kept,
Ghostly figures stir the frost.
Among the pines, the echo leapt,
Of laughter locked away, now lost.

The ghosts of winter gently weep,
Their memories drift through icy air.
In the silence where shadows creep,
Lies a story of love and despair.

Each breath I take fuels the chill,
In this haunt of shadows and light.
Stillness lingers, a deepened thrill,
In the haunted silence of winter night.

Twilight in an Icy Realm

Twilight drapes the world in blue,
As icy breath wraps 'round the trees.
In this realm, all feels anew,
A moment kissed by winter's breeze.

Glistening snowflakes gently hum,
They twirl and dance in fading light.
Nature softly whispers, 'Come,'
To the magic of a starry night.

Frozen rivers shimmer bright,
The sky ignites in lavender hues.
In this ethereal, quiet sight,
The world exhales, its dreams peruse.

Each shadow draped in silver grace,
Steps softly through the velvet gloom.
In this postscript of warm embrace,
The chill cradles winter's bloom.

Time suspends in this tranquil space,
As twilight fades into the night.
In an icy realm, we find our place,
Bathed in the glow of dimming light.

Secrets of the Frozen Ground

Beneath the frost, a story sleeps,
Whispers hidden from the eye.
The earth, in silence, quietly keeps,
All the secrets time can't deny.

Roots entwined with ancient lore,
Buried deep in winter's shroud.
Each layer holds what came before,
In the stillness, the past is loud.

Icy tendrils reach and sway,
Guardians of forgotten dreams.
The frozen ground will not betray,
The tales that linger in moonbeams.

Frosty air bears silent cries,
Of love and loss, of hope and fear.
Every tree creates a disguise,
For hidden stories we hold dear.

In the whispering winds we hear,
The echoes of what lies beneath.
Secrets of the frozen sphere,
Are wrapped in winter's gentle wreath.

Ethereal Mists in the Moonlight

Soft whispers dance in twilight's grace,
As silver beams caress the space.
A veil of dreams, so light and thin,
Where secrets dwell, and stars begin.

Beneath the oak, a shadow lies,
With every breath, the night replies.
The world hangs still, in gentle sway,
As mists embrace the end of day.

Radiant orbs in velvet dark,
Illuminating each hidden spark.
Their glow weaves tales of ancient lore,
Through winding paths, on moonlit shore.

In every corner, silence sings,
Of fleeting time and wondrous things.
Each heartbeat echoes in the night,
As dreams take flight on wings of light.

Ethereal mists, a soft refrain,
Entwine our souls in gentle chain.
With every sigh, the night unfolds,
A tapestry of stories told.

Thawing Hearts Beneath the Ice

Winter's breath, so cold and clear,
Hides the warmth we hold so dear.
Beneath the frost, the embers glow,
Yearning for spring's softening flow.

Upon the lake, reflections break,
As dreams awake, the stillness shake.
With every ray, the ice does melt,
Unraveling hopes that once were felt.

Nature stirs from slumber's deep,
Awakening life from frozen sleep.
In every crack a story lies,
Of whispered love and soft goodbyes.

Buds emerge where silence reigned,
And hearts once closed are now unchained.
A dance of light on shimmering ground,
As joy returns, no longer bound.

Thawing hearts rise up in song,
In harmony where they belong.
Through seasons change, we end our strife,
In warmth reborn, we find our life.

A Solstice Dream in Stillness

The longest night invites the soul,
To ponder deep, to feel whole.
Stars above in quiet glow,
Guide the path where dreamers go.

In promised light, shadows release,
While hearts embrace a sense of peace.
The world awaits in tranquil hush,
As night gives way to morning's blush.

Through shimmering realms where wishes soar,
The solstice whispers, forevermore.
In delicate threads of silver spun,
A tapestry of dreams begun.

Radiance peeks through branches bare,
A reminder that life's always there.
In stillness, find the heart's own song,
Through the night, we all belong.

A solemn promise to carry through,
With every dawn, a life anew.
In quiet moments, joy does gleam,
Awake the hopes within the dream.

Dark Pines Under Twinkling Skies

In shadows deep, the pines do rise,
Their silhouettes against the skies.
Beneath the boughs, a secret sigh,
As starlight spills from pathways high.

The night expands, a velvet cloak,
Each twinkling light, a whispered joke.
Darkness cradles what hearts revere,
In silent woods, we draw near.

Among the roots, the ancients dwell,
In stories wrapped, like a spell.
The wind does carry tales from old,
Of wanderers bold and dreams untold.

In breathless moments, time stands still,
As night reveals a cosmic thrill.
The pine trees sway, a gentle dance,
Inviting all to take a chance.

Dark pines under skies so wide,
Hold secrets close, and fears abide.
In their embrace, we find our way,
As stars above turn night to day.

Frost Flowers in a Frostbite Garden

In the garden, frost does bloom,
Petals spark with silver sheen.
Whispers of the chilly gloom,
Colors bright where none have been.

Ice crystals form a glistening lace,
Nature's art in winter's grasp.
Delicate forms, a soft embrace,
Beauty held in winter's clasp.

Underneath the pale sky's gaze,
They dance in the creeping chill.
In the silence, they amaze,
Holding secrets, quiet and still.

When the sun dares break the night,
Frost flowers fade into air.
Yet in dreams, they shine so bright,
A memory, beyond compare.

In each petal, stories told,
Of winter's kiss and gentle frost.
Frost flowers in gardens of old,
Echoing beauty that won't be lost.

Moonlit Trails of Frozen Paths

Underneath a silver moon,
Trails of frost weave tales untold.
Whispers carried by the tune,
Of the cold, both young and old.

Footsteps crunch on icy ground,
Tracing shadows in the night.
Nature's beauty, so profound,
Illuminated, soft and bright.

Winding paths through trees that gleam,
Silent sentinels of the dark.
In this realm, one might just dream,
Finding solace, finding spark.

Every twist, a story made,
As stars flicker in the sky.
Lost in the beauty, unafraid,
Letting out a gentle sigh.

Where the frozen rivers run,
Guided by the luminous light.
In a world where all is fun,
Moonlit paths stretch out of sight.

Land of the Twilight Snows

In twilight's embrace, snows fall,
A blanket soft, embracing all.
Whispers of warmth, winter's call,
Land of dreams, where memories sprawl.

Shadows play on the silver ground,
Painting a world, serene and bright.
Lost in the magic, joy is found,
In the glow of the fading light.

Mountains high and valleys wide,
Hold the secrets of the cold.
In this stillness, hearts abide,
Sharing stories never told.

Frost clings to branches like lace,
Every flake a tale to spin.
In this land, time leaves no trace,
Moments held, where dreams begin.

As dusk settles on the horizon,
A canvas of colors, soft and rare.
In the land where memories rise on,
Whispers of twilight fill the air.

Dances of the Northern Lights

Above the world, colors collide,
Dances weaving through the night.
Auroras twirl, a cosmic tide,
Painting skies with shades of light.

Whispers of history in the breeze,
Stories etched in shimmering glow.
Nature's rhythm, a gentle tease,
Underneath the stars that flow.

Every flicker, a heartbeat strong,
Echoing dreams from ages past.
In this realm, where souls belong,
Magic moments that forever last.

Beneath the veil, hearts ignite,
Awakened by the timeless dance.
Lost in the beauty, pure delight,
In the night, we take our chance.

As the lights begin to fade,
Memories shimmer in the dark.
In this moment, love is made,
Dances of the northern spark.

Icebound Reflections

In the stillness, ice does gleam,
Whispers of a frozen dream.
Mirror of the pale moonlight,
Every corner shimmers bright.

Trees adorned in crystal lace,
Nature wears a cold embrace.
Footsteps trapped in winter's hold,
Stories of the brave and bold.

Winds of silence gently sweep,
Cradling secrets, soft and deep.
Echoes in the frosty air,
Hushed and frozen, everywhere.

Reflections dance on frozen ponds,
Yearning for forgotten bonds.
Memories in fragments rest,
Held within this icy chest.

Yet beneath, a heartbeat stirs,
Life awakens, gently purrs.
As the thaw begins to play,
Spring will bring a brighter day.

Shadows in the Winter Solstice

Longer nights and shorter days,
Chill of sun-forsaken rays.
Shadows stretch on crisp white snow,
Where the whispering winds do blow.

Fires crackle, warmth ignites,
Gathered close on starry nights.
Stories told in crackling lore,
Binding hearts forevermore.

A silver world of frosty breath,
Hiding life beneath its death.
Yet in silence, seeds will dream,
Awakening to new sunbeams.

The moon, a guardian so bright,
Watches over winter's plight.
In her glow, the spirits dance,
Timeless joy in every chance.

As the longest night draws nigh,
Hope ignites within the sky.
For every dark, a dawn must break,
In the shadows, journeys wake.

Mourning the Autumn's End

Leaves brown and brittle, whisper low,
Crimson tides in the fading glow.
Once ablaze with fiery claim,
Now they fall like silent rain.

Days grow shorter, shadows long,
Nature hums a melancholic song.
Harvest moons begin to wane,
Remnants hold the whispering pain.

Frost will claim the vibrant hues,
Naked branches bid adieus.
Yet in this loss, there's beauty found,
In the cycle, life's profound.

Time flows forward, still we grieve,
For the warmth that we believe.
Yet in mourning, we can see,
A promise of what is to be.

The quiet earth awaits the spring,
In its heart, a living thing.
From the ashes, green will rise,
In the cycle, life defies.

Fading Light Over Snowy Fields

Golden hues stretch across the sky,
As the day begins to die.
Snowy fields, a blanket wide,
Where the fading sunlight hides.

Softly glows the evening's face,
Touching all with gentle grace.
Footprints trail through pale expanse,
Echoes of a fleeting dance.

Whispers rise in twilight's breath,
Life and stillness weave in depth.
Colors melt from day to night,
In the softening twilight light.

Stars will take their rightful place,
In the cold and vast embrace.
Yet beneath the moonlit veil,
Dreams unfold, and hearts set sail.

Each moment, fleeting, yet so bright,
Capturing the fading light.
In the dark, new visions soar,
A journey to forevermore.

Northern Breath of Silence

In the quiet of the night,
Whispers dance upon the breeze.
Stars above, a soothing sight,
Wrapped in winter's gentle freeze.

Pines stand tall, in shadows cast,
Moonlight kisses frosted ground.
Time is still, so calm and vast,
Nature's peace is all around.

Footsteps soft on crisp white sheen,
Echoes fade like distant dreams.
Every breath a silver scene,
In this world of frozen gleams.

Silent lakes reflect the skies,
Mirrors of a tranquil state.
Where the northern breath complies,
With the wonders that await.

Frozen winds tell tales of old,
In the hush, their secrets lie.
Heartfelt stories yet untold,
Beneath the vast expanse, we sigh.

Beneath the Winter Veil

Softly falls the snow so pure,
Blanketing the earth in light.
Nature's quilt, a calm allure,
Cocooned in the hush of night.

Branches bow beneath the weight,
Whispers of a world asleep.
Time slows down, we contemplate,
Promises the silence keeps.

Fires crackle, shadows play,
In the warmth we find our home.
Beneath the winter's white array,
Hearts unite, no need to roam.

Icicles hang like frozen tears,
Glimmers of the chilly air.
In the stillness, calm appears,
Winter's breath, a subtle flare.

Bound by frost, yet free to dream,
Underneath the starry night.
Life may seem like a still stream,
But beneath, it flows with light.

Glaciers' Lament

A distant roar, the ancient ice,
Cracks and groans, a weary sigh.
Once mighty, now pays the price,
Time erodes beneath the sky.

Layers deep, the stories told,
Of earth's past, a frozen art.
In silence, the glaciers fold,
Guardians of the world's cold heart.

Melting dreams in streams of blue,
Whispers of what came before.
A fragile dance of fading hue,
Nature's beauty, evermore.

Echoes of a time gone by,
In the fragments, we recall.
Glaciers' tears beneath the sky,
A solemn truth that binds us all.

In twilight's glow, reflections shine,
Shards of history now exposed.
Through each loss, a hope divine,
In the glacier's tale composed.

Ethereal Caress of Snowflakes

Each snowflake falls with tender grace,
A dance of light, a fleeting dream.
In a world, time holds its place,
Soft whispers in a silver gleam.

Crystals twirl like dancers high,
Spinning under moonlit skies.
A tapestry for the eye,
Crafted by the frost's surprise.

Gentle touch upon the skin,
Nature kisses with a chill.
Innocent and pure within,
Embracing silence, calm and still.

Street lamps glow like orbs of light,
Casting shadows, long and deep.
As the snowflakes take their flight,
Dreamers weave their thoughts in sleep.

Underneath the starry dome,
Winter's breath a lovely hymn.
In this moment, we find home,
In the ethereal, we swim.

Winter's Heartbeat

In the stillness, whispers sigh,
Crystals glisten in the sky.
Trees adorned with cloaks of white,
Embracing the gentle night.

Footsteps crunch on icy ground,
Nature's beauty all around.
Every breath a frosty plume,
Winter sings within the gloom.

Stars twinkle in the northern chill,
A silver light, the world to fill.
Silent shadows dance and play,
As the dawn brings forth the day.

Cabin smoke rises in the air,
Warmth inside, without a care.
Mug of cocoa, cozy cheer,
In winter's heart, we hold so dear.

Beneath the blanket, dreams unfold,
Stories shared, both new and old.
Time slows down, the world feels right,
In winter's heartbeat through the night.

Crystal Dreams

Glistening like stars above,
Nature's artwork born of love.
Frosty whispers on the breeze,
Awakening the sleeping trees.

Each branch wrapped in shimmering lace,
A tranquil charm, a sacred space.
Moonlight drapes the world in white,
Crystals glowing, soft and bright.

Timeless echoes in the cold,
Stories of the brave and bold.
And in the quiet night we find,
Dreams of peace and love entwined.

Glistening paths where shadows dance,
A crystal world, a fleeting chance.
In every flake that falls anew,
Awaits a dream for me and you.

With each breath, the magic flows,
The beauty in the winter glows.
For every heart that dares to dream,
In crystal light, we find our theme.

Glimmers of the Frosted Dawn

As dawn awakens, shadows fade,
A canvas white, a world remade.
Soft hues blush the early light,
Whispers of the stars take flight.

Frosted petals, nature's art,
Glimmers waking every heart.
Every breath a misty sigh,
Underneath the pastel sky.

The world adorned in icy grace,
Morning's kiss on winter's face.
With every step, the silence sings,
Carrying the peace dawn brings.

Birds that chirp, a joyful sound,
In the beauty all around.
Amidst the glimmers, hope is born,
In the hush of a frosted morn.

Golden rays begin to rise,
Chasing shadows from the skies.
In winter's realm, our spirits soar,
Glimmers of the dawn restore.

Echoes Beneath the Ice

Echoes linger in the freeze,
Rippling gently through the trees.
Whispers of a time long past,
In the stillness, shadows cast.

Beneath the crust, a world asleep,
A secret place where dreams do keep.
The icy surface, calm and clear,
Holds the echoes we can hear.

Waves of winter softly hum,
Nature's chorus, a distant drum.
Footsteps taken, memories fade,
But in the frost, they still invade.

Silent waters, stories told,
In frozen depths, a heart of gold.
The echoes dance on winter's breath,
Life persists beyond the death.

Look below, the depth will show,
What lies hidden, soft and slow.
In icy realms, we find our place,
Echoes beneath, a chilling grace.

The Stillness of Winter Nights

The moon hangs low in the midnight sky,
Blanketing fields where the shadows lie.
Silence whispers softly through icy air,
Wrapped in stillness, without a care.

Snowflakes dance on a frosty breeze,
Nature's hush brings the heart to ease.
Stars twinkle bright with a distant glow,
In winter's embrace, peace starts to flow.

Frozen lakes mirror the night above,
A canvas of dreams, so pure, so love.
Echoes linger in the crisp night frame,
As all the world sleeps, calm and tame.

The world slows down in the cold embrace,
Time takes a breath, finds a tranquil space.
Each breath visible in the chilled night,
A moment of breath, a moment of light.

As dawn approaches with whispers of gold,
The night recedes, stories unfold.
Yet in the stillness, memories remain,
Of winter nights, serene and plain.

Hushed Halls of Ice

Beneath the arches of ice, so grand,
Silent corridors, a frozen land.
Whispers echo through the chilling halls,
Where the winter's breath gently calls.

Glistening crystals catch the light,
Fractals of beauty, a wondrous sight.
All is quiet, save for the sound,
Of footsteps softly on frosty ground.

Shadows dance on the sparkling walls,
As moonlight glimmers and gently sprawls.
Time stands still in this frozen maze,
Capturing hearts in a restful daze.

The stillness wraps like a tender shawl,
Embracing everything within its thrall.
In this sanctuary of ice and snow,
The warmth of longing begins to grow.

Yet, solitude carries a gentle grace,
In these hushed halls, we find our place.
Embraced by silence, we come alive,
In the whispers of winter, we truly thrive.

Whispering Pines in White

In the forest deep, where the pines stand tall,
Cloaked in white snow, they shelter all.
Their whispers sway in the crisp, cold air,
Sharing secrets that they hold rare.

Gentle winds weave through the boughs above,
Nature's chorus sings of peace and love.
Sunlight flickers, a spark on the ground,
While the world around is hushed, profound.

Footprints mark paths where wanderers roam,
Beneath the boughs, they find their home.
Every tree tells a tale of time,
In the glistening snow, a perfect rhyme.

A stillness settles, an ancient call,
Where silent echoes softly enthrall.
In the heart of nature, we close our eyes,
As the whispering pines share their lullabies.

Moments enveloped in winter's chill,
In this serene realm, we are still.
Lost in the magic, forever to stay,
In the whispering pines, we find our way.

Midnight in the Frozen Realm

Midnight descends in a world of frost,
Time dances lightly, never lost.
Crystals glitter under starlit gaze,
In the frozen realm where shadows blaze.

A silvered hush blankets the night,
Covering hills in a tranquil light.
Echoes of whispers afloat in the air,
Secrets of night, gentle and rare.

Trees lean closer, branches entwine,
Guardians of dreams in a frozen line.
Each breath visible in the icy air,
In this enchanted world, nothing compares.

As the night deepens, stories unfold,
Of distant dreams and visions bold.
In the realm of frost, hearts soar high,
Beneath the vast, unyielding sky.

With the dawn's approach, stillness remains,
A promise of warmth where love sustains.
In the frozen realm, we find the light,
A midnight journey, peaceful and bright.

A Glimpse of the Northern Star

High above the silent sky,
A diamond glows, a fleeting sigh.
Whispers of the cosmic flight,
Guide the dreams through endless night.

In the chill of winter's breath,
Life and love dance close to death.
Above the world, the star will lead,
In the dark, it plants a seed.

Frozen waves beneath the glow,
Shimmering light on ice and snow.
Through the night, its beacon bright,
Calls the heart to take its flight.

In the quiet, shadows stir,
Echoes of a distant roar.
With each twinkle, hope ignites,
A glimpse of warmth in endless nights.

So gaze upon that starry guide,
Where dreams and wishes will abide.
Hold it close within your heart,
For every journey, it's a part.

Polar Night's Embrace

In the arms of endless night,
Stars are scattered, a soft light.
Whispers travel on the breeze,
Beneath the tall and swaying trees.

Snowflakes dance with silent grace,
Covering the world in lace.
Time stands still, the heart can dream,
Underneath the moon's soft beam.

Each shadow holds a secret tale,
In the night where stars prevail.
Wrapped in warmth, the shadows play,
In Polar nights that guide the way.

The quiet whispers all around,
In the stillness, peace is found.
Wrapped in silence, held so tight,
In the grip of endless night.

Through the dark, the soul can roam,
Finding in the night a home.
Polar night with soft embrace,
Cradles dreams in its warm space.

Frosty Ribbons of Dawn

As night surrenders to the morn,
Frosty ribbons, crisp and worn.
Glistening on the barren ground,
Nature's beauty, softly found.

Colors blush as sunbreaks wake,
Golden hues on winter's lake.
Mist like whispers starts to rise,
Kissing gently, soft goodbyes.

Horizon paints the sky in light,
Hope awakens with the bright.
Each new dawn, a fresh refrain,
Spreading warmth from winter's reign.

Frosty crystals twinkle wide,
In the chill where dreams reside.
Nature's canvas, pure and bright,
Woven through with morning light.

So greet the dawn with open heart,
In each moment, find your part.
Frosty ribbons, a fresh start,
In every dawn, a work of art.

Hushed Frost Upon the Meadow

Hushed frost blankets all below,
Calmly resting, pure as snow.
Whispers linger in the air,
Nature's peace, beyond compare.

Each blade glimmers, kissed by night,
Sparkling softly in dim light.
Life lies still, the world at ease,
Wrapped in warmth beneath the trees.

Morning sun begins to rise,
Bidding farewell to starry skies.
Frosty petals glisten bright,
Waking up to pure delight.

In this hush, the world can breathe,
Every moment pure, we weave.
When frost touches earth's sweet face,
It brings a quiet, stunning grace.

So walk the meadow, feel the chill,
In this magic, hearts can fill.
Hushed frost whispers where we tread,
In every step, life gently led.

Quartz Crystals of the North

In the stillness, they gleam bright,
Whispers of time in the moonlight.
Angles sharp, secrets held tight,
Nature's art, a stunning sight.

Crafted by ice, silent and fair,
Each facet catches the cold air.
Stories etched in their clear stare,
Magic woven into their glare.

Rivers flow beneath their core,
Ancient echoes forever roar.
Glistening in a winter's lore,
Quartz crystals, we do adore.

Beneath the snow, a radiant glow,
Life beneath layers, waiting to show.
In the silence, thoughts drift slow,
Nature's touch, so deep and low.

Guides to a world that's often lost,
Beauty that comes at a great cost.
In the north, where the air is frost,
Quartz crystals, a path embossed.

Nature's Breath of Quietude

In the woods, a gentle sigh,
Leaves whisper secrets floating by.
Silent moments under the sky,
Nature's breath, a lullaby.

Moss blankets the forest floor,
Trees stand tall, wisdom they store.
Every sound a chance to explore,
Echoes of life in the core.

Birds take flight with soft wingbeats,
Dew-misted dawns, the heart greets.
Sunlight dances where silence meets,
Embracing the peace that entreats.

Clouds drift slowly above our heads,
Time suspended, nothing dreads.
In the quiet, emotion spreads,
Nature's voice, where calmness treads.

Soft rustle, a breeze that lightly stirs,
Whispering tales only the heart concurs.
In this haven, each moment infers,
A symphony where stillness blurs.

The Last Leaves of Autumn

Golden remnants cling to the bough,
A fleeting beauty, here and now.
Softly they dance, take their bow,
Whispers of change, time to allow.

Crisp air carries a scent of gold,
A story of seasons, gently told.
Nature's canvas, vibrant and bold,
As leaves surrender, their fate unfolds.

Beneath the trees, a carpet grows,
Crimson, amber, in cheerful rows.
Nature's promise, each gust bestows,
A wondrous cycle, life's love shows.

With each flutter, memories fade,
Past warmth lingered, now just a shade.
In the twilight, the silence wades,
Awaiting winter's cool cascade.

Soon, the branches will wear white coats,
But for now, the last leaf floats.
In the breeze, a heart still gloats,
For autumn's charm, forever emotes.

Winter's Canvas of Still Life

Blankets of white drape the ground,
A world transformed, peace profound.
In silence, solitude is found,
Winter's art, so pure, renowned.

Frosted branches gleam like beams,
In the quiet, all softly dreams.
Reflections dance on icy streams,
Nature's beauty, or so it seems.

Footprints mark a solitary trail,
In the stillness, whispers prevail.
Nature's breath, a whispered tale,
Through winter nights, we knit and sail.

Stars above in a velvet sky,
Shimmer like hopes that never die.
With each flake, the moments fly,
In the magic, we learn to fly.

The chill brings warmth within our souls,
In winter's grip, we seek our goals.
Life's canvas painted, love consoles,
In this quiet, the heart extols.

The Dance of the Northern Gale

In twilight's embrace, they swirl and sway,
The northern gales in a frosty ballet.
Whispers of snowflakes, a crystalline tune,
They glide through the pines, beneath the pale moon.

Echoes of laughter, the night feels so bright,
As shadows of starlings take graceful flight.
The chill in the air offers sweet, tender charms,
While frost-kissed trees wave with open arms.

Each gust a caress, a lover's soft breath,
Painting the landscape, a canvas of death.
Yet life is a dance in this winter's delight,
As long as the gales roam beneath the night.

The world transforms gently, a silvery dress,
Nature's own magic, a frosty caress.
With each swirling whisper, the night weaves its thread,
A dance of the northern winds, softly spread.

So let us join in, with hearts open wide,
To sway with the gale, our spirits as guide.
With the cold all around, let warmth still prevail,
As we lose ourselves in the dance of the gale.

Breath of the Arctic Evening

In twilight's hush, the air breathes deep,
An Arctic evening, where shadows creep.
The world holds its breath, as time stands still,
Wrapped in serenity, a quiet thrill.

Beneath the vast sky, stars shimmer bright,
Reflecting on ice, a magical sight.
A whisper of wind brings stories untold,
Of glaciers and mountains, both timeless and bold.

The aurora dances, a canvas of fire,
Painting the heavens, a luminescent choir.
Colors entwine, like dreams made of light,
Illuminating the heart of the endless night.

Soft flakes cascade, like memories past,
Each one unique, a treasure to last.
In the silence, I breathe in the night,
Embracing the chill, my spirit takes flight.

The Arctic evening sings a sweet song,
Where the quiet prevails and I feel I belong.
In the breath of the cold, I find my true way,
In harmony with nature, forever to stay.

Moonlit Glades of White

In moonlit glades, the snowflakes gleam,
Blanketing earth like a distant dream.
Silent and pure, the night whispers low,
Through trees dressed in white, with a gentle glow.

Footsteps muffled in the soft, fresh snow,
A sparkling wonderland with secrets to show.
Each flake tells a story, unique and bright,
Illuminated softly by the pale moonlight.

The air is crisp, with a stillness divine,
Nature's peace wraps around, so finely entwined.
Underneath the stars, I find my own way,
In the moonlit glades where my heart longs to stay.

The branches reach out, like arms in embrace,
Inviting me softly to find my own place.
Amongst the white wonder, with dreams taking flight,
I wander the night in a dance of delight.

So here in the moonlight, I feel the embrace,
Of nature's soft beauty, a tranquil space.
In the glades of white, peace takes its soft hold,
As the night whispers secrets, both tender and bold.

The Quiet of a Frosted Dawn

As dawn breaks slowly, a hush in the air,
The frost gently glimmers, its beauty so rare.
The world wakes in silence, a delicate sight,
A canvas of silver kissed by first light.

Each blade of grass wears a crown made of ice,
Reflecting the sun's golden, warm slice.
In this tranquil moment, time seems to pause,
Embracing the quiet, nature's own laws.

Birds stir from slumber, their songs fill the scene,
Echoing softly, a melody serene.
The trees stand proud, draped in frost's embrace,
As warmth starts to rise in this peaceful space.

With every soft breath, the dawn takes its cue,
Painting the horizon in shades fresh and new.
In the stillness, I find a sacred song,
The quiet of dawn, where my heart feels strong.

So let me remain in this moment so pure,
Where the frost meets the light, it feels right and sure.
In the quiet of dawn, new beginnings arise,
As the world gently wakes beneath pastel skies.

The Yearning Heart of Winter

Whispers of frost dance in the air,
Hearts wrapped in silence, dreams laid bare.
Each flake a memory, softly it falls,
Winter's embrace in the stillness calls.

Bitter winds weave through the sighing pines,
Echoes of warmth in flickering lines.
Candlelit windows with laughter inside,
While the yearning heart learns how to bide.

The moon hangs low, a silvered thread,
Casting shadows where whispers tread.
A symphony played by the night so deep,
In the arms of winter, secrets we keep.

Stars blink softly in the velvet sky,
Time slows down, as moments fly by.
In the chill of the night, our spirits unite,
With the yearning heart, we embrace the light.

As dawn breaks softly, painting the scene,
A canvas of white, the world in between.
The heart of winter, though cold, still beats,
In the dance of the snow, our longing completes.

Nightfall Over the Frozen Lake

The sky dips low, a blanket of night,
Reflections shimmer, silver and bright.
The lake lies still, a mirror of dreams,
Where silence hums with the night's quiet themes.

Stars twinkle down like diamonds tossed,
In this serene world, no joy is lost.
The air is crisp, a breath of pure peace,
As gentle whispers coax the stillness to cease.

Moonlight spills softly, a luminous hue,
Illuminating shadows, where darkness once grew.
The frozen expanse holds stories untold,
Where every reflection breathes yearning and bold.

In the hush of the night, serenity hums,
A melody sweet as the still water comes.
Each ripple, a secret, a moment in time,
Residing in echoes, a lyrical rhyme.

As night weaves its spell, the world falls in place,
A haven of dreams draped in still grace.
Over the frozen lake, peace takes its stand,
Bathed in the magic of night's gentle hand.

Lament of the Bare Trees

Naked branches reach for the clouded sky,
Their whispers of sorrow echo and sigh.
Once clothed in laughter, now cloaked in cold,
Bones of the forest, their stories unfold.

Seasons have changed, yet they stand alone,
Guardians of memories, roots set like stone.
Through storms and stillness, they bide their time,
In the breath of the wind, they cradle their rhyme.

Each twig like a finger tracing the past,
In every rustle, a tale unsurpassed.
Frost-kissed and weary, yet resilient they stay,
In the depth of winter, they dream of the May.

Ghosts of the blossoms long gone from the grove,
Burden of winter, yet pulse with love.
For every lost leaf, a promise is sown,
In the heart of the bare, the green is not gone.

Lament of the trees mingles soft with the night,
A vigil of patience awaiting the light.
With roots intertwined, they ground their despair,
In the stillness of winter, their strength is laid bare.

Veins of Ice in the Wilderness

Across the expanse where the wild winds blow,
Veins of ice shimmer, a delicate glow.
Paths of the frozen, marked by the cold,
Whispering tales of the brave and the bold.

Nature adorned in a crystalline lace,
Silent and fierce in its drifting embrace.
The trees stand tall, dressed in frozen dreams,
Guardians of beauty in silence, it seems.

Mountains whisper secrets to the biting air,
In the heart of the ice, resilience is bare.
With every heartbeat, the wilderness strives,
Veins of ice pulse where the winter survives.

A canvas of white, where shadows now play,
Under the moonlight, the spirits sway.
The wild is alive with the chill of the night,
In the veins of ice, there's warmth in the white.

As dawn breaks anew, the chill starts to fade,
The wilderness stirs, hidden paths are laid.
Veins of ice may shimmer, yet life remains true,
In the heart of the wild, every moment's anew.

Memories of a Frosted Horizon

Beneath the pale, winter's glow,
Whispers of the past still flow.
Frozen breath in biting air,
Moments linger, precious, rare.

Echoes dance on crystal streams,
Captured softly in our dreams.
Footprints traced in powdery snow,
Time stands still, yet we must go.

Branches draped in icy lace,
Nature's art in still embrace.
Frosted fields where shadows play,
Memories bloom, then fade away.

Stars above in silent watch,
Guiding hearts with every notch.
In the chill, a warmth we find,
Threads of love forever bind.

Glacial Serenity in a Sea of White

In a world of muted tones,
Silence reigns, and peace is grown.
Mountains rise with snow-clad crowns,
Nature wears her crystal gowns.

Footfalls soft on frosted ground,
Echoes of a soft profound.
Breath of winter, pure and clear,
Glacial beauty, drawing near.

Winds that weave through barren trees,
Carry secrets, gentle breeze.
In this realm, the heart finds space,
In the stillness, find our grace.

Colors fade to shades of gray,
Underneath a sky of clay.
Every flake adds to the scene,
In this quiet, all serene.

Frost-laden Air and Hearts Unbound

Frost hangs heavy on the boughs,
Nature whispers, takes her vows.
Underneath a quilt of white,
Hearts awaken, feeling light.

Every breath a fleeting cloud,
Silent moments, peaceful, proud.
As we wander, hand in hand,
In this magic, we will stand.

Each soft step on snowy ground,
Softened echoes, a sweet sound.
In the chill, our spirits soar,
Frost-laden air, we yearn for more.

Stars reflect on icy streams,
Woven tales from whispered dreams.
In this realm, we find our place,
Hearts unbound in winter's grace.

Tapestries of the Wintry Wilderness

A canvas pure of fine white snow,
Nature weaves a tale below.
Branches bow with frozen grace,
Each flake kissed with time's embrace.

Crisp air carries distant calls,
Through the woods where comfort falls.
Twilight paints the world in gray,
As shadows dance and softly sway.

Textures blend in nature's hand,
Life unfolds upon the land.
Every drape of white we see,
Hints at stories yet to be.

Amidst the stillness, hearts can dream,
In the quiet, find our seam.
Tapestries whose threads unite,
Wintry wonders in the night.

Veiled in Silver Lace

Moonlight drapes the quiet land,
Whispers of night, gentle and grand.
Stars twinkle like diamonds in space,
Nature dons her veiled silver lace.

Trees stand tall in frozen stance,
Beneath their branches, shadows dance.
The world feels still, caught in embrace,
Lost in dreams of a starry place.

Soft snowflakes drift from skies above,
Like feathered whispers of winter's love.
Every breath, a misty trace,
In the heart of this silvered grace.

Silhouettes waltz in the night's cool air,
Under the moon's watchful stare.
Silent secrets time cannot erase,
Held tightly in this silver lace.

With each dawn, the beauty will fade,
Yet memories linger, never betrayed.
For in winter's chill, there lies a space,
Forever captured in silver lace.

Echoes of the Frozen Stream

In the heart of winter's chill,
A stream runs silent, calm, and still.
Its waters weave through time and trees,
Echoes linger, carried by the breeze.

Beneath a veil of frosted white,
Memories dance in the pale moonlight.
Nature's song, a soft, sweet theme,
Carried forth on the frozen stream.

Footprints mark the snowy shore,
Tales of wanderers, and much more.
With every breath, a silent dream,
A world alive by the frozen stream.

Ice crystals form a sparkling crown,
As winter whispers, stealing the sound.
Yet in this quiet, there's a gleam,
Life persists in the frozen stream.

As spring approaches, the ice will yield,
And secrets of the past revealed.
Yet the echoes of a soft, sweet theme,
Will linger on from the frozen stream.

Beneath the Crystal Blanket

A world transformed, pristine and bright,
Wrapped in layers of white delight.
The earth, it sleeps, in silence profound,
Beneath the crystal blanket, wrapped around.

Footsteps crunch on the powdered ground,
With every step, a joyous sound.
Nature rests under winter's dome,
In this embrace, it finds its home.

Stars pierce through the frost-filled night,
Glowing softly, a comforting sight.
While dawn unfolds, a golden beam,
Breaks the hush of the crystal theme.

Time slows down in the frosty air,
Each moment cherished, a wondrous prayer.
The world feels soft, like a sweet dream,
Held gently beneath the crystal blanket's gleam.

Seasons will change and time will pass,
Yet beauty lingers, a shimmering glass.
For in our hearts, winter's always supreme,
Beneath the warmth of a crystal dream.

Cries of the Winter Wolf

Through the shadows of the night,
Calls a creature, fierce and bright.
A haunting echo, wild and deep,
The cries of the winter wolf, they seep.

In silvered woods where silence reigns,
Ghostly figures dance in the plains.
With fur like snow and eyes that gleam,
Awakens the moon in a haunting dream.

A pack united, strong and bold,
In the darkest night, their stories unfold.
Through frost-kissed air, their voices stream,
A chorus rising, wild, yet serene.

Each call tells tales of ancient lore,
Of moonlit hunts and windswept shore.
In the heart of winter, they find their theme,
The cries of the winter wolf, a primal scream.

Nature watches, timeless and wise,
As the echoes drift beneath starlit skies.
With every heartbeat, hearts will dream,
To the low howls of the winter wolf's theme.

Solitude of the Frozen Peaks

In the stillness high, the mountains breathe,
Cloaked in white where silence weaves.
Nature whispers secrets old,
In the grasp of winter's hold.

Each flake a story, softly told,
Under skies of cobalt gold.
With every gust, the echoes fade,
In solitude, the heart is laid.

Glistening heights, a frozen throng,
They sing of sorrow, they sing of song.
In the crack of dawn, the world awakes,
To embrace the peace that stillness makes.

Trails of dreams where few have trod,
A path unmarked, a snowy facade.
Here in the quiet, one finds a spark,
Of life anew in the frigid dark.

Beneath the peaks, the soul finds grace,
In a ceaseless, solitary space.
With every breath of icy air,
The frozen peaks reveal a prayer.

Resilience in the Icy Silence

Snowflakes dance on whispering winds,
In the calm where the battle begins.
Frozen grounds hold stories deep,
Of strength and courage, stark yet sweet.

Amidst the chill, the heart takes flight,
Finding warmth in the pale moonlight.
Roots push through the hardened cold,
In every crevice, life unfolds.

Silent strength beneath the frost,
In each moment, never lost.
Against the storms, a spirit bold,
Resilient tales of warmth retold.

With every breath of crisp, cold air,
Hope springs forth, fragile yet rare.
In the icy silence, life persists,
A testament of those who insist.

From barren remains, new dreams will rise,
In the hush where determination lies.
Nature teaches through frost and snow,
The resilience within us continues to grow.

Muffled Footsteps on Shimmering Snow

In the hush of night, footsteps blend,
With the soft sighs that the cold winds send.
Each step a whisper, soft and light,
On shimmering paths kissed by the night.

Cold crystals glimmer underfoot,
Silent paths where the wild things hoot.
Every trace a tale of wonder,
Beneath the stars, the world is under.

Moonlit shadows play and hide,
In this frosty realm where dreams abide.
Muffled sounds wrapped in the chill,
Marking places where spirits thrill.

With every step, the world feels near,
In the soft embrace, there's nothing to fear.
Wind and snow become my guide,
Through the night, with stars as my pride.

Muffled footsteps in silver light,
Lead me deeper into the night.
In the shimmering glow, I find my way,
Embracing peace as night turns to day.

Secrets Held by the Winter Moon

In the night, the secrets bloom,
Bathed in light of the winter moon.
Silvery beams on silent hills,
Whisper tales that the heart fulfills.

The air is crisp, a shiver runs,
As stars wink softly, one by one.
In the stillness, shadows play,
Guarding truths that drift away.

Winds carry echoes from the past,
Through the trees, where shadows cast.
Each glimmer holds a silent scream,
Wrapped in frost, a fragile dream.

Beneath the moon, the world lays bare,
In the stillness, secrets flare.
Embrace the night, let it weave,
Mysteries that the heart believes.

The winter moon, a watchful eye,
Witnessing dreams as they glide by.
In its glow, we find our fate,
As the cold whispers, it's never too late.

Shadows of the Frosted Moon

Under the frost's soft embrace,
Shadows dance in quiet grace.
Whispers of night through the trees,
Moonlight flickers with a breeze.

Silent echoes of forgotten dreams,
Veiled in silver, quiet gleams.
Each footstep breaks the frozen air,
Lost in wonder, unaware.

Reflections glisten on the pond,
As stars above the earth respond.
Night's calm holds a gentle sway,
Where shadows linger, night and day.

Beneath this vast and endless sky,
The world beneath begins to sigh.
Frosted whispers call me near,
In every echo, I find cheer.

A tapestry of cold and light,
Painted veils on this deep night.
As the moon drapes its silver thread,
With shadows where my path has led.

Wistful Wanderings on Ice

In morning's glow, the world stands still,
A canvas white, a magic thrill.
Footprints trace a path so clear,
Wandering thoughts of yesteryear.

Each breath releases a frosty sigh,
Beneath the vast, uncharted sky.
Wistful whispers on the breeze,
Carry tales through silent trees.

Crystals sparkling on frozen streams,
Merging past with future dreams.
I skate through moments, soft as snow,
Embracing all, both high and low.

The heart finds warmth in chilly air,
As we dance without a care.
Memories swirl like flurries bright,
In the embrace of winter's light.

Each glide a journey, each turn a tale,
Through frozen fields where memories sail.
Wistful wanderings, soft and slow,
In a winter's dream, I choose to flow.

Veil of Icy Mist

A shroud of white envelops the ground,
In a world where silence can be found.
Fingers of frost caress the dawn,
As nature awakens, dreams are drawn.

Mist weaves patterns, soft and dim,
A ghostly dance, a haunting hymn.
Through this veil, the spirits glide,
In harmony, they whisper wide.

Branches adorned with icy lace,
The breath of winter holds its grace.
In this beauty, shadows play,
While the morn begins its gentle sway.

Hidden pathways come alive,
In the stillness, hopes survive.
I tread softly through the gloom,
Awake to dreams that start to bloom.

Veil of mist, you cloak the sun,
Yet reveal the magic, every run.
Through icy realms, my spirit roams,
In the heart of nature, I feel at home.

Song of the Winter Winds

Cold winds carry a haunting song,
Through valleys deep and mountains strong.
With every gust, there comes a tale,
Of distant lands where dreams set sail.

Whispers glide on frosty breath,
Echoing life, yet hinting death.
Through barren trees, their fingers spread,
A symphony of the silent dead.

In swirling gusts, the memories play,
Of summers past, in vibrant sway.
Through winter's grasp, the echoes call,
Of warmth and laughter within the fall.

Winds weave softly, cradling night,
Illuminating the starry sight.
A dance of shadows, flickering light,
In the song of winter, taking flight.

Beneath the stars, I stand enthralled,
Listening to the winds, so called.
In every note, a story blends,
The song of winter never ends.

Reflection in the Snow

The world is wrapped in purest white,
Soft blankets cover earth from sight.
Footsteps echo on the path,
As silence speaks, a gentle wrath.

Mirrored skies, a tranquil hue,
Glimmers shine, a world anew.
Every flake, a whispered story,
In winter's chill, we find our glory.

Bare trees stretch to touch the clouds,
Nature dressed in snowy shrouds.
Reflections dance in frosted streams,
Carried softly on winter's dreams.

The stillness reigns through evening's glow,
While icy winds begin to blow.
A moment paused, we breathe it in,
Finding warmth where cold has been.

As twilight falls, shadows play,
Inviting night to take the day.
In dreams of silver, hearts drift slow,
Embracing peace in the falling snow.

Frosty Dreams and Starry Skies

Underneath a velvet dome,
Stars awaken, far from home.
Frosty air and breath so light,
Chasing dreams through starry night.

Sapphire skies hold secrets tight,
Whispers of the coming light.
Each twinkle holds a tale untold,
In winter's clasp, pure stories unfold.

The moon reflects on icy streams,
Painting paths of soft moonbeams.
Crisp and clear, the world lies still,
Beneath a blanket, soft and chill.

Wanderlust calls through frost-kissed air,
Inviting hearts without a care.
Through quiet woods, we roam and glide,
With starlit dreams, let's take the ride.

As dawn arrives with blush and fire,
We chase our hopes, we chase desire.
Frosty dreams and skies so bright,
Fill our souls with pure delight.

Lonesome Paths of Winter

Footsteps lead through drifts of white,
A lonesome journey, quiet night.
Each breath a cloud in frigid air,
Nature's beauty, stark and rare.

Bare branches stretch to catch the moon,
In winter's grasp, the world in tune.
A solitary path unfolds,
As stories of the cold are told.

A distant sound, the owl's soft call,
Echoes through the frosty hall.
While silence blankets every form,
The heart feels warm against the storm.

Shadows dance with shimmering light,
Casting dreams into the night.
These lonesome paths, though cold and bare,
Hold whispers of the beauty there.

In every step, a moment found,
In winter's heart, love does abound.
Though alone, I'm never lost,
For in this chill, warmth's worth the cost.

A Whisper Across the Tundra

Through stretches vast, the tundra glows,
A whisper flows where cold wind blows.
   Soft murmurings of ancient lore,
   Echoing tales of the land before.

   Icicles hang like crystal spears,
  Guarding secrets of countless years.
A world untouched, both fierce and free,
   In winter's arms, we find our glee.

   The sky, a canvas bold and bright,
     Painted hues at dusk, in flight.
   Each star a promise, gently cast,
  In moments lived, they hold us fast.

Across the plains where shadows creep,
    Silent stillness in silence deep.
  A whisper calls through endless night,
   Binding hearts with pure delight.

   As dawn awakens frozen ground,
   In every heartbeat, love is found.
  For in the frozen wild's embrace,
  We find our truth, our sacred space.

The Quiet Between Snowflakes

Softly falls the silent snow,
Whispers linger, hush below.
Each flake dances, unique and light,
Cradled softly in the night.

Footsteps fade on frosted ground,
In this peace, stillness found.
Moonlight glimmers on the white,
Crafting shadows, pure delight.

Crisp air hums a gentle tune,
Underneath the silver moon.
Embracing warmth in cold's embrace,
Time slows here, we find our place.

Blankets wrap the weary earth,
In this calm, there's silent mirth.
Nature holds her breath so dear,
In the quiet, we draw near.

Moments linger, softly bound,
Lost in thought, without a sound.
Here in winter's gentle grace,
The quiet sings, a sacred space.

Echoes of Ice and Silence

Crystalline echoes fill the air,
Ice reflects the winter's glare.
Silence weaves a fragile thread,
Where whispered thoughts and dreams are bred.

Frozen branches arch and sway,
Guarding secrets of the day.
Moments captured, time on hold,
Stories waiting to be told.

Glistening blankets cloak the ground,
In this stillness, peace is found.
Every breath a quiet song,
In the hush, we all belong.

Windows frost with tales of old,
Memories in whispers told.
Beneath the weight of ice and night,
Hearts ignite with softest light.

Here, in spaces vast and wide,
We find warmth where dreams collide.
Echoes drift through silent skies,
In the still, our spirits rise.

Beneath the Polar Sky

Underneath the polar glow,
Stars like diamonds softly flow.
Painting dreams in hues of night,
Guiding souls with gentle light.

Snowflakes twirl and dance around,
Whispered secrets, tender sound.
Each a promise, soft and bright,
In the canvas of the night.

Frosty winds, they sing a tune,
Beneath the watchful, crescent moon.
Dreamers gather, hearts align,
Lost in magic, moment divine.

Here the world feels vast and free,
Wrapped in warmth, just you and me.
Underneath the polar sky,
We'll chase wishes, let them fly.

In these moments, time will bend,
As we wander, hand in hand.
Embracing wonders, we can find,
Love shines brightest, unconfined.

Solstice Gaze

In the chill of winter's breath,
We gather close, defying death.
The solstice whispers ancient lore,
Promising light forevermore.

Fires crackle, shadows play,
Welcoming the returning day.
As darkness wanes, our spirits rise,
Beneath the ever-changing skies.

Candles flicker, warmth awakes,
Stories shared, the heart remakes.
In this circle, love ignites,
Guiding us through longest nights.

Hope unfurls like tender leaves,
In the light, the soul believes.
With each flicker, every gaze,
We dance through the solstice haze.

Together here, we find our way,
As twilight fades to break of day.
With joy we welcome what will come,
In the light, we are all one.

A Solemn Gaze Toward the Sky

In twilight's hush, the stars align,
A whispered wish, a distant sign.
Clouds drift slow in evening's grace,
I find my peace in a solemn gaze.

The moonlight spills on fields of night,
Casting shadows, soft and white.
Each twinkle tells a tale untold,
Of dreams that shimmer, brave and bold.

With every breath, the silence grows,
Nature's symphony, sweetly flows.
A timeless bond, with skies above,
I seek the warmth of fleeting love.

Beneath the dome of endless blue,
My heart reflects the vastness too.
In moments still, I dare to fly,
On hopeful wings, toward the sky.

Ethereal light, a gentle guide,
Through night's embrace, where secrets hide.
A solemn gaze, a whispered sigh,
Together we dream, you and I.

Journey Through the Arctic Moon

In shadows deep, the icy breath,
A frozen path, where whispers rest.
Beneath the glow of silver light,
I tread softly, through the night.

The Arctic winds, they sing a song,
Of ancient tales, where spirits throng.
Each step a dance on crystal tiles,
Guided by dreams across the miles.

The auroras paint the sky so bright,
A dazzling canvas, pure delight.
With every flicker, a journey unfolds,
Revealing secrets that time holds.

In this realm of tranquil freeze,
My heart finds solace, a gentle ease.
The moonlit path, a guiding star,
Leading me home, no matter how far.

The echoes of the night collide,
As I walk on, with hope as my guide.
In this frozen land, I roam free,
A journey through eternity.

Frost-kissed Memories

In morning's light, the world awakes,
A quilt of white, the silence breaks.
Each frosty breath, a memory spun,
Whispers of warmth from days long gone.

The crunch of snow beneath my feet,
A symphony of winter's beat.
With every step, the past unfolds,
In silver shades, our stories told.

The trees adorned in diamond lace,
Hold echoes of a sweet embrace.
Frost-kissed wonders linger long,
A gentle tune, a sacred song.

In light's caress, the shadows play,
With every hue, they fade away.
Yet in my heart, they'll always stay,
Frost-kissed memories, come what may.

Though seasons change, and time moves on,
The frosty gems will not be gone.
They linger softly, pure and bright,
In whispered dreams of the winter's night.

Delectable Frost on Maple Branches

On maple branches, frost delights,
Glistening under morning lights.
Each crystal gem, a sweet surprise,
A treat for all enchanted eyes.

Beneath the weight of winter's kiss,
The world is wrapped in snowy bliss.
Nature's art, a masterpiece,
In every flake, a moment's peace.

With gentle breath, the cold air sings,
As frosted leaves do dance on springs.
Delicate forms, so still, so bright,
A fleeting joy in purest white.

In silence lies the magic spun,
A tapestry of chill and sun.
Each maple branch, a story sung,
In whispers soft, where hearts are young.

When spring arrives, the frost will fade,
Yet in my heart, those glimmers laid.
Delectable dreams on branches high,
Forever etched in memory's sky.

Milton Keynes UK
Ingram Content Group UK Ltd.
UKHW010229111224
452348UK00011B/615